Dysfunctional Families

The Truth Behind
the Happy Family Facade

Katherine Mayfield

ISBN # 978-0-9976121-2-7

First print edition published by The Essential Word.

Also by Katherine Mayfield

*Stand Your Ground: How to Cope with a Dysfunctional Family
and Recover from Trauma*

The Box of Daughter: Healing the Authentic Self

*Bullied: Why You Feel Bad Inside and
What to Do About It*

*Dysfunctional Families: Healing the Legacy
of Toxic Parents*

The Box of Daughter and Other Poems

The Meandering Muse

*What's Your Story?: A Quick Guide
to Writing Your Memoir*

Smart Actors, Foolish Choices

*Acting A to Z: A Young Person's Guide
to a Stage or Screen Career*

Praise for Katherine Mayfield's Work

"Katherine Mayfield holds nothing back, and her unflinching, thorough, and articulate honesty is a true gift for anyone wanting to understand, face, and rise above the emotional scars of a damaging childhood."
—Amy Wood, Psy.D., author of *Life Your Way*

"...A testament to the merit of psychological healing through the understanding and expression of feelings."
—Kirkus Reviews

"Well-written, intriguing, and so very enlightening!"
—LibraryThing

"Fresh, bold, and inspiring."
—Examiner.com

"A compelling and insightful expose of the damage bullying can do to a child's self-esteem, and of measures that can be taken to stop it....For anyone who ever found themselves at the mercy of a bully, Mayfield's latest offering is definitely a book to have front and center on your shelves."
—*Nashua Telegraph*

To Emma

Contents

Recovery

Spirituality

Why I Wrote This Book

Between 2005 and 2008, I was the family caregiver for my parents. During those years, I met numerous other caregivers who were struggling under the heavy burden of caregiving in dysfunctional families. I began writing a series of blogs on Life in a Dysfunctional Family, describing some of the insights I gained from the experience of living in a very dysfunctional family for almost 50 years, and offering encouragement and suggestions for healing based on my own journey of recovery from emotional pain. This book is a compilation of some of those blogs and other pieces of writing on dysfunctional families that have surged out of my writer's mind over the years.

One of the hallmarks of dysfunctional family systems is secrecy, and this tradition of concealment affects every area of family members' lives—not only relationships, but also careers, money, friendships, and values. I hope that by sharing my insights in these essays, I can provide inspiration to help you pull the veil of illusion away from your eyes so you can see yourself, your life, and your family more clearly.

Growing up in a dysfunctional family can be a very negative influence on a person's self-esteem. In my case, I grew up thinking I was worthless and helpless, despite fairly regular evidence to the contrary. Over the course of twenty years, I dug down deep inside of myself to find out who I really was underneath all of the disapproving messages and constricting beliefs that I had grown up with, and began a wonderful journey to freedom in which I rediscovered my authentic self.

Every human being is magnificent, and everyone has a valuable talent to offer the world—but most of us are taught to compress our authentic selves into a tiny compartment in order to conform to society's expectations, and sometimes to make our parents happy, and we lose sight of the potential we have to do great things.

Here you'll find essays on subjects ranging from end-of-life issues (if you're caregiving), coping with your emotions, and suggestions for living more authentically, to overcoming old money habits, building your self-esteem, and deepening your spiritual life. I hope you find relief from the issues that aggravate you, and discover heaps of your authentic self as you read.

Katherine Mayfield

Spider Love

I've recently been rereading Martha Beck's amazing book, *Steering by Starlight*, and again I'm struck by how clearly she describes love as it's often experienced in dysfunctional families.

In the book, Ms. Beck makes an analogy between a spider who builds a web so it can catch flies and suck the life out of them, and what she calls "Spider Love," where someone traps others in webs of obligation so that they can feed off of them emotionally. That's exactly what happened in my family.

When I first read Ms. Beck's description of "Spider Love" (p. 196-7), I nearly fell over. Throughout all those years the life was being sucked out of me, I didn't notice, because I was taught to believe instead that I wasn't good enough, that I didn't do enough, that I must be defective and stupid if I couldn't make my family members happy.

In retrospect, though, I realize that they were feeding themselves with my attention, my desperate attempts to give them what they wanted, and the emotional gyrations I went through in response to the guilt and criticism they threw at me. They didn't really want to be happy, they just enjoyed their power over me, and the web was strengthened every time I hoped for their respect and encouragement, and didn't receive it.

Spider Love can happen in any relationship: family of origin, romantic liaison, friendship. Any time you feel as if the number of choices you have in a relationship are getting smaller and smaller and smaller, or that *you're* getting smaller and smaller and smaller, you're probably experiencing Spider Love.

Along with therapy, what helped me most to overcome Spider Love was learning how to give encouragement to myself, so that I couldn't get hooked into a relationship where I was always hoping that validation would come from the other person. It felt really odd at first—mostly because it was so unfamiliar—but it's a great tool to have in my self-help repertoire, because now I can get encouragement any time I need it! I still enjoy being encouraged by other people, but now I don't depend on it for my self-esteem.

The only hand you will hold throughout your life is your own. So start giving yourself some encouragement!

Maybe It's Not You

My parents were often critical of me. And it got worse as they got older.

They judged my values, my beliefs, my abilities, and most of my actions to be deficient or incorrect, unless I was doing exactly what they thought I should do. They often reminded me that their way of doing things was the right way, and unless I followed their lead, I was wrong. This is a major pattern in many dysfunctional families, and it left me with very little self-esteem.

It wasn't until my parents were gone that I could start taking a clear look at the whole situation. For one thing, they were grounded in a lifestyle that worked for people sixty years ago. Their generation saw more world change than any other to date, and they had a hard time keeping up with the times. They did the best they could, but the strain was obvious.

And as they aged, they needed to exert more effort to feel like they were in control of themselves. One of the ways they did that was to put me down and bully me. It made them feel powerful and more in control.

Along the way, I developed the belief that I wasn't good enough, that I didn't know how to cope with life, that I wasn't very smart, and that I did everything wrong. But that was only because I thought they must be telling the truth. After all, they were my parents.

When people age, and it seems like their bodies are letting them down and their minds are not as sharp as they used to be, they sometimes turn to criticism as a way to feel like they still have some power in life. It doesn't always mean that the people they're criticizing are doing anything wrong; sometimes it just means the criticizer is desperately trying to hang on to his or her own sense of self. In fact, people of any age may resort to criticism and bullying to gain a sense of power when they're feeling weak or lacking themselves. But criticizing someone doesn't take into account the fact that none of us can walk in each other's shoes. No one knows what it's really like inside another person, or what's best for someone else.

So if you're struggling under the weight of a lot of criticism, do some reality checks with trusted friends or other family members. Ask them if they see the same kinds of issues in your life. You might discover that maybe the real problem is not you after all.

Criticizing is easy. Looking within, coping with the ambiguity of life in a mature way, and growing into your potential is not. Some people prefer the easy way.

Unwilling Martyr

Somehow, I ended up with the role of the Giver in my family. I don't know how it happened.

I do believe in giving—giving from the heart, and giving with love—but being an Unwilling Martyr is really neither of those.

Growing up with two narcissistic parents, there was no room for any needs that I might have. I didn't even know I had any needs at all until I got to the middle of my life—I thought only other people had them, and I wasn't supposed to, so I pushed them so far back into my mind that I forgot about them.

My parents needed so much of my attention and energy that I didn't have enough left over to get my own life going. Every time I tried, every time I made a step forward or reached a goal or started working toward something positive in my own life, they dragged me back into taking care of them. Such is the nature of a codependent relationship. They were so afraid of sticking their own necks out that they didn't want me to stick mine out. They just wanted me to take care of them.

Growing up in a dysfunctional family can mess up your life in a big way. Usually, the biggest part of the problem is that most children who grow up in a dysfunctional family have very low self-esteem, so it's difficult to see themselves in any kind of positive, life-affirming way. That's what happened to me, even though I was the Giver. In the beginning, I wanted to give. But over the years, it changed until it felt like everything was being taken, rather than my actually choosing to give, because no one could hear me say, "No."

Nothing that I did was ever good enough. Looking back, I can see so clearly that I gave, and gave, and gave, until I was sick and emaciated and had absolutely nothing left of myself. I was totally drained. How is it that I could never see myself as a good person? That I could never say, "I've done enough, it's my turn"? That's part of what goes on in dysfunctional families. Whatever you do, it's never enough.

Well, I'm here to say, Yes, it is enough! When you've given a lot to members of your family over the years, and you haven't gotten much support back, maybe it's time to rethink the situation. If you're the Giver, and you've had enough, you can be very sure that you're a good person, because of all you've given over the years. You might want to check out a book on narcissistic people, like *Why Is It Always About You?* or *Trapped in the Mirror*. Both these books helped me understand the situation and reclaim some of my self-esteem.

If you've been the Giver all of your life, think about how you might feel differently if the situation was reversed—if someone was eager to give you everything you wanted. What would your life be like? Who would you perceive yourself to be? Or, how would everything be different if you gave as much to yourself as you always have to other people?

We all deserve to be taken care of, to be appreciated, to feel welcome in the world. Even if you have to give that to yourself, it can change your life in a big way. If you're not comfortable receiving, do some meditation to find out why.

Unwilling Martyrdom is one of the most lethal dysfunctional family patterns there are. If you want to become more of who you really are, you need to lift up this label and figure out exactly what is going on under it.

Disobeying the Status Quo

I discovered one day that my life wasn't going anywhere because I had picked up the habit of "keeping the status quo" from my parents. They liked things to stay pretty much the same—they very clearly gave me the unspoken message "Don't stick your neck out." But on the day I realized that I had mimicked their habit, I also realized that the other name for "Don't stick your neck out" is "Live in a rut where nothing ever changes."

Having lived way too many years in that same rut, I finally decided to climb out of it and move forward. But from deep within, a tiny voice cried out, "We can't do that!" I've discovered that listening to those tiny voices inside, and asking them what they're talking about, has led me to some of the most amazing insights—real awakenings about some of the destructive messages I received as a child—and has also helped me to let go of those old beliefs and behavior patterns that hold me back, that aren't part of who I really am.

As I listened inside for what that voice was really trying to communicate, I discovered that it was afraid of disobeying. As a survivor of emotional abuse, and a witness to physical abuse in my family, it has taken me decades to feel comfortable going my own way rather than following my parents' rules, and as I thought about that tiny voice, I realized that moving forward would have constituted "disobeying" in my parents' eyes, and years ago, would have resulted in punishment for not doing what they wanted.

So after my parents passed away, I decided I would have to disobey them if I wanted to create a life that is truly my own.

It wasn't easy. Every time I tried to step forward, parts of my psyche that were formed early in childhood got really scared. I had to keep reminding those parts of myself that my parents were gone, and would never come back to hurt me again.

I finally figured out that I could move forward if I acknowledged that yes, I was going to feel like I was disobeying, but I was going to go ahead and find myself anyway. And I was happy to find that I didn't get in trouble at all. In fact, my life seems to work a lot better—probably because I'm doing things in the way that works best for me, not following someone else's rules or advice.

Sometimes we have to disobey those old childhood messages—and even the messages we get from society—before we can begin to discover the authentic self that lies underneath the "false self" that always had to follow the rules.

That's when the magic starts to happen.

Let Me Have My Own Life, Please

My dad was really into investing. When I went to visit, he would pull out his files and graphs and show me everything he was doing, and I listened, because it was the only thing he wanted to talk about, and I wanted to connect with him. Over the years of listening, I learned quite a bit about investing, and started investing my small savings here and there.

A few years ago, we were talking on the phone, and I mentioned an investment I wanted to make. He didn't agree with my choice, and we got into an argument that ended with him saying, "You don't know anything about investing!" Rather than seeing immediately that this wasn't true—after all, he had taught me everything he knew—the part of me that was still unsure of myself believed him, and I didn't make the investment. My trust in myself and my abilities plummeted, because I had let him talk me out of believing in myself.

When I was thirteen, my parents gave me $25 to buy some clothes. It was my first chance to buy something I liked, all on my own, with no parental influence. I found a beautiful silk shirt on sale, in a color that looked fabulous on me. I took it home to show my mother, and she said, "You don't want that, do you?" I spent the rest of the money on books.

Because my parents were more interested in having me reflect their own tastes than in helping me develop as an individual, they put me down and belittled my choices, time after time, until I didn't know who I was any more.

It's taken me many years to learn to trust myself again, to see that when someone has an agenda, they will often try to talk you out of your own perceptions. Manipulative people will discount your perceptions because they want things their own way. But just because someone else thinks they know better than you what's right for you doesn't mean that they do. Sometimes they're just seeking validation for their own beliefs and desires.

Each one of us has the right to perceive things however we wish. If someone is trying to invalidate your perceptions, they probably don't have your best interests at heart. I was taught when I was a child to trust those in authority—but after five decades of seeing my life screwed up every time I relied on someone else's judgment, I've finally learned to trust myself, and my life has gotten so much better.

The Drama Addiction

When I was a child growing up in the Midwest, I learned that life was about drama. My mother was very impulsive, and our daily life changed a lot depending on her whims. Some days she was up, and life looked great. But when she was down, everything was a catastrophe. Spilling a bit of milk wouldn't make her cry, but it sure sent the mercury on the irritation thermometer up about 50 degrees.

As an adult, I've had to "unlearn" the habit of dramatizing every little difficulty in my life. The problem with being addicted to drama is that even when things are generally going well, I end up focusing on some small detail that's out of place or slightly off, and by keeping my focus on problems, pretty soon I have more of them. Then I'm back in the place where everything is a catastrophe, and the cycle starts all over again.

Having a life like a soap opera provides a certain high, a certain thrust of energy, sometimes even the motivation we need to keep moving forward. It gives our brains something that they love: a problem to solve! Even if all you really want is peace, when you're used to drama, a peaceful life can seem dull and boring.

The first step in achieving peace and letting go of the addiction is to notice when you're spiraling into it. If it doesn't involve death or a visit to the hospital, tell yourself it's not worth getting upset about. It takes practice, like any skill, but you truly can make your way to a peaceful life if you work on breaking your addiction to drama.

Drama addiction is a hallmark of dysfunctional families. People in dysfunctional families often catastrophize in order to avoid dealing with the real underlying problems of the family's dynamics. You don't need to live in a state of constant drama. The secret is to say to yourself, "So what? Will it really matter next year, or next week?" And then let it go.

By detaching from the drama of problems, you can allow peace to grow within you, and let the drama enter instead into the beauty, joy, and freedom that you want to create in your life.

There are many excellent books on codependence and dysfunctional families. An easy and informative read to start with is *The Drama of the Gifted Child: The Search for the True Self*, by Alice Miller. This book will show you who you really are.

Beyond the Drama Addiction

So, are there any benefits to overcoming the Drama Addiction? You bet there are.

The number one benefit I discovered is that I have much more time and energy to start creating an exciting and fulfilling life because I'm not spending all my focus and attention on drama.

Here's a comparison: Sally, a Drama Addict, consistently (and unconsciously) creates tension in her life by getting upset over any event that doesn't turn out the way she expects it to. She grew up in a drama-addicted family, so that's all she knows. She and her partner are going out for a nice dinner and dancing, and on the way to the restaurant, they get stuck in a snarl of traffic caused by work that's being done on a burst sewer pipe. After two minutes of sitting in a long line of traffic, Sally begins to feel frustrated and angry, as if the world is out to get her, and the feeling escalates into an assertion that nothing ever goes her way and she never gets anything she wants. Her partner picks up on her energy, and the evening starts to get tense. Three minutes later, they're on their way, but the evening has been ruined by Sally's unconscious tendency to dramatize everything. Dinner is not very much fun, and they decide to skip the dancing. By the time they get home, Sally is exhausted after focusing all evening on her anger and frustration.

Contrast that picture with Anna, who is not addicted to drama. (Anna must have grown up in a relatively functional family.) In the same situation, Anna and her partner use the five minutes in traffic to talk about possibilities for a day trip they want to take the next weekend. There are few distractions, so they are able to be focused and listen to one another's ideas and desires, and by the time the traffic moves again, they've decided on a destination. When Anna gets home, she's energized and excited, and starts to plan the trip.

Another major benefit of giving up dramatizing is that it reduces stress and allows more room for moments of contentment and peace. It's also easier to overcome problems, because they won't seem so huge, and your thinking will be much clearer as well.

Most people who are addicted to drama grew up with a lot of drama in their families of origin, but sometimes people dramatize because they're afraid of stepping out and creating a truly exciting life. The drama can make life seem exciting, even though it's really more about feeling frustrated and overwhelmed.

If this is true for you, remember that small risks often have to be taken in order to grow, and by taking small risks, you can meet your need for drama and grow at the same time. If you don't have any supportive people who encourage you to reach out and take some risks and grab life on your own terms, find some. Get some new friends or a new community, or find a good counselor.

And when you find yourself getting overly upset about some small thing, remember that it's only a habit, and consciously turn your attention to something you'd rather have in your life. Instead of dramatizing, you could try cooking a new food or going to a new restaurant to add some spice to your life.

Is there something you always wanted to explore, but felt you never had the time to try? If you stop dramatizing, you'll find the time. Take a dance class, visit a museum, learn a language, plan a trip. Write your life story. Start to integrate some real excitement into your life, and you'll begin to drop the drama habit. On the way, you'll be creating a much better life for yourself.

That Old Black Magic

It happened again.

One day, I woke up and found that I had fallen back into my old ways: wanting to control everything, being fearful of the future, and afraid to try anything new, even when my intuition was trying like heck to help me keep moving forward in my life.

My brain spewed out my old beliefs: "No matter how hard I work, I'll never get what I want, and even if I do, somehow someone will take it all away." (That one goes back to my relationship with my mother.) "I'm incapable of handling life." (That one's still in there, in spite of nearly 30 years' worth of evidence to the contrary.) "I can't trust anyone or anything." That's the one that made me realize I'd fallen back into the old, rusty, tangled mess of insignificance and uncertainty where I spent so many years of my life.

It's that old black-magic spiral. I can move forward for months in a positive direction, and then something comes along that knocks me back into my 10-year-old head, and I start spiraling down, down, down into the depths of ancient and deep-rooted negativities. But I've finally accepted that it's going to happen now and then—as much as I try to focus on the positive, sometimes those old computer settings in my brain get activated, and my former beliefs and behaviors step right into the spotlight.

It took me about 24 hours to figure out why I dropped back into that old place in my brain: someone close to me had put me down in an attempt to make herself feel bigger. It was subtle, but that was the trigger. If I ask myself often enough, "How did I get back here?", eventually the answer comes. It just takes a little time and determination to ferret it out.

What's important when we fall back into old patterns is to take the time to figure out why, to let the insights we've learned over the years come back to the forefront, and to focus, focus, focus once again on what we want to believe, and what we choose to create, instead of berating ourselves for repeating mistakes—because we *do* have a hand in creating our own reality, but when we abdicate that power, the subconscious takes over in creating our reality, and we're back to the same old, same old.

What do you want to create in your life? Fight those old demons like a warrior, and know that though they may return now and then to haunt you, you are bigger and more powerful than they are, and the future is not determined by the past, unless you allow it to be.

The Financial Abyss

As I write this, the U.S. national debt is more than $15 trillion. Although my own debt was never that high, I can really relate. For many years, I had problems with money. In spite of inheriting a fierce frugality compulsion from my Depression-era parents, underearning and debting always felt more like "the real me" than being financially stable did.

I read every book on money that I could get my hands on: books on visualizing, overcoming underearning, thinking like a millionaire, creating money energetically, having the courage to be rich. But that tradition of never having enough stuck to me like superglue. No matter how hard I worked, my life seemed to be locked into "Poor Little Match Girl" mode.

After my father passed away, my rabid focus on money in relation to the work that I do grew arms and legs, sprouting into every corner of my life. I kept thinking, detach, detach, detach; let it flow, let it flow.

But it didn't.

As I grappled with conquering one dysfunctional family pattern after another, my perspective began to shift, and my life juddered along with it. Eventually, all of the insights I gathered about the tangled web that was my understanding of money and work dovetailed, and exploded into one radiant revelation: my desire for money wasn't actually a desire for money; at its root, it was a craving for my father's acknowledgment. Since I'd never received the acknowledgment of the person who controlled the money in our family, I couldn't let myself receive money. I had always thought of money as synonymous with my father—because it was his jurisdiction—and I was still waiting for his permission to have enough.

I had visited my parents once a year in their old age, and every time, my father would sit me down with his investment statements and hand-drawn stock charts between us, and talk for as long as I would let him about how the stock market worked, how he made his investment choices, and why he decided to draw his charts in their particular ways.

The first few times, I tried to interject comments here and there which I hoped would keep a flow of conversation going, but my remarks were usually ignored or brushed aside. I was reduced to saying, "Mm-hmm," "I see," and "Oh, your chart looks nice" for hours, until I escaped to the bathroom to get away.

This wasn't a conversation. This was teacher and student, monarch and peasant, master and slave. This was full-blown Spider Love, as described by Martha Beck in her wonderful book, *Steering by Starlight*.

I must admit I learned quite a bit about investing from our talks over the years, but the most powerful lesson I took away was that I was not worthy of having opinions, my affairs were not worthy of discussion, and I was not worthy of any attention at all in terms of the financial realm.

Year after year, I sat listening to my father as if I was chained to the chair with a gag in my mouth, trapped by my compassion—by my knowledge that I was the only one who really listened to him. My mother's attention needs were even more ravenous than his, and consequently, she soaked up so much attention that there was rarely any left for him. He had very few friends, so these tortuous (for me) "investment talks" were the only time someone really listened to him.

Throughout my life, I was my father's teddy bear—the one who was always there for him. And teddy bears don't make any money.

It took me three and a half years after his death to see our relationship for what it truly was. My father was a good and gentle man, volunteering and giving wherever he could, but there was a hole inside of him, an inner anguish that nothing could assuage, no matter what he achieved or how hard I tried to help.

In my attempt to fill his emotional void, I created a money hole in my own life in the form of debt, putting plane trips for parental visits on credit cards because I didn't want to spend my hard-earned money to go, and taking time off from work that I couldn't really afford in order to go and pay attention to my parents. I didn't want to, but over time their pleas and entreaties to go and visit them would become louder and stronger and more insistent, until I would finally go just to shut them up for awhile.

The Unwilling Martyr was at it again.

I wonder: is our fervent national pursuit of more, better, bigger really, at its root, a quest for acknowledgment? For someone important to say, "Yes. You are worthy of attention. Your needs are important. You're doing a great job with your life!"

For the children of Depression-era parents, who grew up in an atmosphere where profound fear of loss fused with no clue as to how to offer acknowledgment, the quest for money can be linked deep in the psyche with unmet emotional needs. Once the truth is unearthed, and the feelings expressed, we can let go of the compulsion that never really quite satisfies.

Does Money Grow on Trees?

Money doesn't grow on trees, at least in America. But so many new herbs and amazing cures for specific diseases have been found in various rainforests that it makes me wonder if there might be a couple of money trees way back in there, spewing out dollars that are just waiting for the Federal Reserve Board to show up with a special vacuum and suck them all up.

Life After Caregiving

There is life after caregiving. As much as we love those who are close to us and want to make them as comfortable as possible during the last years of their lives, once they've moved on, we need to grieve, let go, and reenter our lives.

Caregiving for elderly parents can be one of the most difficult processes in life. But it does come to an end, even though you may not be able to see or feel that when you're in the middle of it. I hope the following essays help you through your experience and offer comfort in some small way as you travel through this turbulent time.

There is Life After Caregiving

Caregiver burnout is not a myth. After caregiving for my parents for more than seven years, by the time they passed away I had lost so much weight from the stress, I was down to 100 pounds. I had given all my attention to helping my parents and I was in a state of near-collapse. (My memoir, *The Box of Daughter*, tells the story of my relationship with my parents.)

I noticed lots of resources for caregivers during those years, but never took much time to investigate them. I was too busy worrying and feeling responsible, being the "good little girl" I was supposed to be.

My parents had been demanding all of their lives, and as they grew older, they relied on me more and more. Some part of me saw their end-of-life processes as my last chance to please them, to finally satisfy the demands they had thrown at me for so many years, so it seemed imperative to give every ounce that I could. In spite of it all, they both died unfulfilled and unhappy, and it took me quite awhile to understand that their dissatisfaction with life had nothing at all to do with me.

Caregiving is one of the few experiences in my life that, looking back on it, I would have done differently. I would have made a grab for all the caregiver resources I could find, swallowed my pride and asked for help, and paid more attention to my body's early signals of tiredness and distress. I would have given myself a break by pursuing things that I enjoy and paying more attention to having fun, rather than worrying constantly about my parents.

Most of all, I wish I'd found a way to put my parents' dying process in perspective. After all, death is a normal part of life. My father was in hospice for the last eight months of his life, and during our last visit, I finally understood how detrimental my relationship with my parents had been in relation to my sense of self. At that point, I could have started really paying attention to myself and avoided the decline in my health, but I was already burned out and couldn't see any other way. I just kept worrying and trying to make everything better for my father. There's a point at which you can do nothing more for someone who's in the process of moving on; the trick is to figure out when that is, and to stop worrying and just "be there."

Though I loved my parents and wanted to give them the best care that I could, it's a relief to have my life back. I've regained my sanity by reminding myself that it's okay to be healthy and happy, it's okay to pay attention to my needs, and that peace can finally be restored to my life. I've discovered there is life after caregiving, and that I deserve to focus on my own life, my own goals, and my own health with as much determination as I focused on helping my parents in their last years.

If you're a caregiver, ask for help. It just might save your your sanity—and your life.

Post-Funeral Detox

While some people may grieve from the heart after a family member's passing, those of us who were raised in very dysfunctional families may experience something more akin to a mental / emotional detox. This is okay. The guilt that can come up surrounding the process of letting go of a painful relationship is part of the old gunk we need to let go of.

It's not a sin to feel relief when someone with whom you've had a difficult relationship passes away. It's a normal human reaction to being released from tension and conflict.

If you find yourself wanting to detox after the loss of a painful relationship, the most powerful thing you can do is to find a way to express all of your thoughts and feelings so that you can achieve closure on the relationship. Get a photo of the person, or sit down across from an empty chair, and imagine that they are there, unable to speak. You have all the space you need to express your feelings. Tell the person everything about how you felt and what you wished had been different.

One of the hallmarks of very dysfunctional families is that there's not often any kind of resolution to conflict—it just goes on and on. So you need to resolve it for yourself. You need closure on the relationship. Therapy can be very helpful if the relationship has been very toxic. Bereavement groups can also help you detox.

Here are more suggestions to help you through:

- Do as many nice things for yourself as you can in the days following the funeral. You don't have to try to have fun (unless that feels right), but you can buy yourself flowers, take naps, pursue your favorite activities, sleep in, eat your favorite foods.

- Pick an item that you received from the person who passed away—an item that perhaps you never liked, but felt obligated to keep or display—and choose a charity to give it to. As you give it, imagine the obligation, guilt, and pain that you felt in that relationship dissolve and float away.
- On the left side of a piece of paper, draw a picture of what the relationship was like for you, how it made you feel, what it may have made you do that you wouldn't have done otherwise. On the right side, draw a picture of how you feel now, or how you want to feel as you recover from the relationship. Feel free to use words and symbols. Even if you're like me and can't really draw, this is a powerful exercise.
- Turn your favorite music on, and do a victory dance. You survived, and you're free now to live your life you own way.

This kind of emotional work can be very difficult. But if you don't make an effort to release the old feelings and attain closure, the unexpressed feelings will make it feel like the relationship is still going on, long after the actual person has passed away. You may have looked forward to freedom for a long time—this is your way to claim it.

If there were aspects of the person or the relationship that you loved and enjoyed, acknowledge that as well. Many family relationships are a mix of love and irritation, in differing amounts.

I wish you peace in your recovery, and joy in finding your true self!

Life Force Energy Debt

During the seven years I acted as caregiver for my parents, my energy was constantly going out: talking with doctors and nurses, investigating medications, trying to give my parents the support they needed in a difficult time.

After my mother died in 2005, my focus went to my father—helping him through his loss, trying to make up for my mother's absence, and hunting for anything, anything, that would make him more comfortable as he descended into dementia. By the time he passed away in 2008, I was totally burned out.

Then came the process of sorting through their possessions and settling the estate. More energy going out. By the time it was finally finished, I had developed a massive habit of putting energy out without taking much in, and I ended up with an enormous life force energy debt.

It's been two years now, and only recently have I realized that with all the demands of caregiving, I'd forgotten how to take energy in. Eating became very important during those years—it was the primary way to replenish myself. Breathing and exercise were helpful, too, but as soon as I stopped one of these helpful activities, I'd go back to putting energy out at 100 miles an hour.

A few weeks ago, I was taking a walk on a late fall morning, and as I turned my face to the sun, I noticed its lovely light glinting on the surface of a nearby pond. Beautiful, I thought to myself, and then I lunged forward again in my quest for nourishing exercise. Something stopped me, compelled me to turn back and look at the moving lights on the water, and I realized that I hadn't even taken in the splendor of the scene.

I stood and breathed in the glory of Nature at her finest, and at that moment, a wall dropped inside of me. As I took in the sparkle of the sun on the water, for the first time in many years, I felt energy coming in through my pores, my eyes, my ears, my hands, my skin. The Universe was flooding me with chi, with life force energy—always there, always available. All I had to do was stop and take it in.

As caregivers, we often close the doors of our energy system to keep out the pain, but we're also shutting out the energy of the Universe, which plentifully provides for our sustenance.

As I've continued to practice taking in energy this way, I've found many more opportunities for nourishing myself. Everywhere I go, I look for what I can take in. Though I never liked chores like grocery shopping, now I enjoy strolling down the aisles, looking at all the colors and shapes and patterns, taking in the energy of food without even eating. And I feel fed and nourished, on every level—by the colors, the diversity of products, the sheer numbers of possibilities for creating meals.

Caregiving is a life-wrenching process, but even when you're putting out huge amounts of energy, there's chi everywhere, just waiting to feed you if you take it in.

Caregiver Guilt...and All That Jazz

You feel like you just can't do enough for your 84-year-old mother.

Monday, it's a new medication. You stop on the way home from work to pick up the prescription.

Tuesday, there's a new symptom. You call the doctor to schedule an appointment.

Wednesday, your mother is depressed and keeps you on the phone for an hour, needing your support.

Thursday is the appointment to get a new pair of eyeglasses, because she's not seeing very well lately.

Friday, she falls and sprains her wrist. Does it ever end?

As much as you (probably) love your parent and want to do everything you can for him or her, the fact is that elderly people need a lot of care, and if you try to take care of all their needs yourself, you risk running your own health into the ground.

When I was caregiving for my parents, my biggest problem was guilt. Even though I took care of every need I possibly could, it still felt like it wasn't enough. That's because I couldn't reverse the aging process for them—I couldn't make their joints work like new, I couldn't give them back the foods they used to love and couldn't eat any longer, I couldn't give them back the energy or the positive outlook they'd had when they were younger. I couldn't assuage the sorrow that losing health and vitality inevitably brings to the aging.

But I finally realized that my guilt was counter-productive. It doubled the weight I was carrying. I couldn't change the reality of my parents' aging, and there was only so much I could do for them.

Guilt is really just a habit. I decided to develop a counter-habit of reminding myself (and it took concentrated practice) that my guilt wasn't doing anybody any good, that it wasn't helping the situation, and that I didn't need to go there. I finally broke the guilt habit. And when I got most of it out of the way, I found I could respond more from my heart instead of my head.

Moving beyond guilt actually makes a better caregiver, and helps the caregiver take better care of self. Do yourself a favor and get some help and support during this difficult time. Make sure you're taking care of yourself—you deserve to have as much care as you need, too.

No, Really, We're Fine

Recently, a friend of mine lost her uncle. He was in his eighties, and she's been the sole caregiver for him for the last six years. Though he was fairly functional up 'til the end, a lot of her time, energy, and attention went to make sure he was getting his needs met—doing his grocery shopping, picking up prescriptions, visiting at least once a day to make sure he was okay.

When he went into the hospital a few days before he passed away, he kept saying, "Everything is fine. I'm ready to go back home," even though he had been complaining to my friend for years about how bad things were, and he was obviously very near the end.

It reminded me of my mother, who years ago when she was in her eighties, complained constantly that she needed help with the house, the chores, the grocery shopping, everything. I couldn't help because I lived more than 1,000 miles away, so I suggested contacting an elder agency for help. She thought it was a great idea.

Imagine my surprise when I took my parents to the agency on one of my visits, and my mother told the intake counselor, "Everything is just fine. We don't have any problems. We don't need any help." She just couldn't be vulnerable with someone outside the family. Shortly after that, my parents moved into assisted living.

The current generation of elderly people was brought up to be completely self-sufficient, relying on family whenever help was needed. So that's the public façade they present, even when they feel life is falling down around them. Though they may seem extremely needy to family members, they deny to the world at large that they need help, and this can be very confusing for caregivers.

Often, this is the first time that a caregiver needs to overrule a parent's wishes. If the caregiver cannot provide for the family member's care, he or she needs to find an agency that can. Every state has some form of elder care assistance, and a caregiver need not feel guilty for taking advantage of them—that's what they're there for.

It's extremely important for caregivers to keep their own needs in mind, to care for themselves as well as their elders. I've been there, and I can tell you, if you don't take care of yourself, your own health can suffer terribly. My friend landed in the hospital a few weeks ago, totally burned out from having to care for her uncle on top of making a living and keeping her own life together. The same thing nearly happened to me.

Even though you may never have felt it, you are just as important as the person you're caregiving for. Get some help before the burden becomes overwhelming.

Father's Day

As Father's Day arrives, I'm reminded of the time I spent going through my father's effects after his death, feeling really guilty that I probably hadn't done as much for him in the last years of his life as I should have, in spite of feeling like I did everything I possibly could.

I opened one of his desk drawers and discovered piles of cards—Father's Day cards, birthday cards, Christmas and Easter and Thanksgiving and Halloween cards—that I sent to him when I wasn't visiting. In looking at those cards, all the things I *did* do for him suddenly came to the front of my mind. Along with the cards, there were many phone calls, packages of gifts, even calls to the nursing home staff to get an objective view of how he was doing when I needed some perspective.

I imagined him opening the drawer full of cards when he felt lonely or needed a lift. The guilt lessened as I noticed within the stack of cards the presence of my caring for him over time, of letting him know again and again that I thought about him, that I loved him, and that he had a special place in my life, even if I wasn't by his side.

I reminded myself that even if I felt like I wasn't doing enough, I did the best I could, and I know I made a real difference in his life. Whether or not he thought I did enough, I was there for him when he needed me.

End-of-Life Service

I got the call on a Sunday afternoon in April, 2005.

"You'd better come," the director of the nursing home told me. At 89, my mother had been diagnosed with ovarian cancer six weeks earlier, and she also had heart problems. The director indicated that she was showing signs of getting ready to go.

I flew to Illinois the next morning, and my mother sat up in bed when I walked into the room, but she was clearly not in very good shape: restless, anxious, unable to settle. Over the next 24 hours, I spent as much time as I could with her, talking, comforting, praying.

The following afternoon, the minister at the nursing home suggested to my father and me that she'd like to perform an End-of-Life service, the Protestant version of last rites. We agreed, and an hour later we gathered in my mother's room. The service was simple but beautiful, offering thanks for my mother's life and prayers for her journey.

What I remember most vividly is a section where the minister told her that we could walk with her to the gates of heaven, but no further. My mother kept saying, "It's so beautiful." Her voice and her body were peaceful for the first time since I'd arrived—more peaceful than I had really ever seen her at all—and I sensed an eagerness in my mother to live in a place of such beauty. The service provided a superb container through which we could all acknowledge our feelings and say goodbye.

My mother passed away very early the next morning, totally at peace.

I highly recommend some kind of End-of-Life service when the time comes. It offered all of us, each in our own way, the opportunity to come to terms with the fact that my mother would be journeying to a new life and that my father and I might continue on, but that as a family, we were no longer a unit. It allowed my father and me to separate from my mother and let her go, and I think it gave her the permission she needed to leave us and move on to the next stage of her journey.

Most importantly for me, it provided a tremendous sense of closure, not only for my relationship with her, but for the long and difficult process of her aging and death, a process which we had shared for many years.

Family ties can be incredibly strong. Formalizing the natural occurrence of death in some way can give permission to the dying to let go, and permission to the living to go on living.

Time to Move On

I remember the last time I visited my father in the nursing home before he died. Even with dementia, he still knew who I was, and the moment I walked in the door, he criticized my choice of clothing. I thought he'd be glad to see me, but I guess the Critical Habit gets pretty ingrained by the age of 92.

It wasn't surprising; my family was extremely dysfunctional, and every time my parents were at a loss for words, they criticized whatever seemed appropriate at the time. Yet I felt so sorry for him, because it was obvious how much he was suffering.

One of the most difficult aspects of caregiving for very elderly people, I think, is the feeling of how powerless you are to make things better for them, because you know that whatever you do, the person is still going to suffer.

In my humble opinion, the medical system keeps some people alive way beyond the point at which they have a good quality of life. Both of my parents suffered tremendously in the last few years of their lives, and both were kept alive, against their own wishes, by the medications the doctor prescribed. That's not the way they wanted it—they had always been very clear that they didn't want life prolonged by medical intervention, and had even finalized all the paperwork. The paperwork covered resuscitation and methods for keeping them alive in the event of an emergency, but it said nothing about medication. And by law, the nursing home could not discontinue his medication.

Shortly after my visit, my father called the funeral home director and asked about euthanasia. Even with dementia, he was extremely clear that he didn't want to live any longer. He lived for almost a year after that.

Please let me go when it's my time, don't keep me here to suffer just because a pill will keep my heart going or unclog my arteries. When I'm old enough and there's nothing more to look forward to, I want to move on.

Taking Care of Yourself

It's vital to figure out how to take care of yourself when you're caregiving. After years of caregiving for my parents, in the last eight months of my father's life I became so exhausted that I went from 118 pounds down to nearly 100 (I'm 5'5", so I'm even thin at 118).

I had all kinds of tests and saw several specialists, but we couldn't find a reason for the weight loss. I was eating more than I'd ever eaten in my life, in an effort to stay energized, but my body wasn't absorbing the food. I looked like a skeleton. My friends started getting worried, and I had to pin pleats in my pants. It was truly frightening.

I know now that it was simply exhaustion and the stress of caregiving, because within two months of my father's passing, I started gaining weight, and I gained it all back within three months. Looking back on it, I think it was my body's way of telling me that I was literally disappearing under the weight of all the worry and responsibility.

If I had it to do over again, I would have done whatever I needed to do to get more support, and not tried to do everything myself; I would have let go of the guilt that was useless but was eating away at me (sometimes there is truly nothing you can do to make the situation better for someone); and I would have asked for help in detaching from the situation, for death is inevitable, after all. I hope my experience will serve as an example of what not to do when you're a caregiver.

The Dream is the Revealer

About fourteen months after my father passed away, I dreamed that he had been living with me, though I never saw him. I only knew he was living in my space because I saw his shoes, and the newspaper was always open to his favorite page: the financials. His presence permeated every corner of my living space. It was as if he had always lived with me.

In the dream, one day I came home, and he was gone. All of his things had been removed, and his presence had evaporated. I woke with the realization that I had carried him in my psyche for a long time, and that I'd finally achieved enough peace about the difficulties of his last years that I could let him go.

The dream helped me to realize that I needed to let go of my identity as caregiver. For more than seven years, my caregiving experience had been so engulfing that I sort of forgot that it's not an integral part of who I am.

Feelings that I had to repress in order to be a good caregiver surfaced in the years after my parents died: leftover frustration at not being able to relieve their suffering, some resentment at how much of my own life I had to put aside, and sadness at the impending loss and the general difficulties of aging and the death process. I wasn't able to express those feelings while I was caring for my parents, but after they were gone those emotions bubbled up, wanting to be released. It was a comfort to finally have the time and attention to let go of it all, and for me, it was a very important part of the grieving process.

An experience as profound as long-term caregiving doesn't just dissolve when it's over so that everything can go back to normal. There are feelings to process, and sometimes it takes a conscious decision to look at all of it and let it go.

The dream helped me to release the energy of emotions that had been pent up for many years, and begin to move on. It helped me realize it was time to begin looking forward to the rest of my life.

Embrace Your Inner Gargoyle

I recently read a great little book called *Owning Your Own Shadow* by Jungian analyst Robert A. Johnson. After dealing with my dysfunctional family for so many years, I have a massive shadow which follows me around like a giant lizard from Jurassic Park, tripping me up with its obstacles and changing my brain's interpretation of reality into scenes from my childhood.

After twenty years (off and on) of weekly visits to the therapist's office, I've shrunk my shadow from XXXL down to a size eight, but I still struggle occasionally with anger, frustration, and fear related to my past.

What I loved about *Owning Your Own Shadow* was that the author offers practical suggestions for integrating the shadow into one's life in manageable ways, rather than continuing to shove it under the rug so it blurts out at the most inopportune and inappropriate times, like when you're trying to make points with your boss or mother-in-law.

According to Johnson, if we refuse to acknowledge our individual shadow, it can manifest as depression, psycho-somatic illness, and a tendency toward accidents. He stresses the need to acknowledge that there's a dark side to the psyche which can't be ignored.

Since the dawn of time, various cultures have expressed the shadow in bloodletting rituals and sacrifice to keep it from invading daily life, but in the Western world, we expect everything to be good and light. Our repressed and unacknowledged collective shadow bursts out in economic difficulties, war, political upheaval, and racial intolerance.

The more we try to repress and ignore the shadow, the stronger it gets. I imagine that criminals and murderers must have gigantic, insatiable shadows. My own shadow generally expresses itself in sudden bursts of anger and frustration at really small stuff, and also with regular dribbles and spills of various foods and liquids as I fix meals in the kitchen. When I ignore the signs and try to control things even more, they just get worse.

Johnson refers to his suggestions for integrating the shadow as "shadow upkeep." He cites one couple who assigned the task of taking out the garbage to whoever had enjoyed the most good fortune that week, as an attempt to give expression to the darker side so it doesn't interfere with the light of joy. Other ways to express shadow energy could be cleaning, weeding, painting, writing, or dancing the shadow. My own favorite is grabbing a sofa cushion, gritting my teeth, and shaking it for all it's worth, usually while imagining a particular person from childhood in its place. Then I dust off the cushion and fluff it up before I put it back. Even small silly acts like this can relieve huge amounts of tension.

Now, when a forkful of cat food clatters to the floor or the kitchen spray hose hits me in the stomach, I think to myself, "That's the shadow," and remind myself that I'd rather have my shadow energy express itself that way than erupt into a much larger disaster. When I'm feeling frustrated with life, I clench my jaw and growl and shake my head, imagining the shadow within becoming a gargoyle for a few seconds. Then I can go back to my life feeling a little calmer, a little cleaner, a little more in control. When the inner darkness has been fed, there's a little more light. My psyche's balance has been restored.

Johnson suggests that the shadow also contains gold—the highest and most honorable qualities in ourselves that we were taught to repress or disclaim in modesty—and that the gold can be even more terrifying to us than the darkness. *Owning Your Own Shadow* is a short, easy read, but offers a goldmine of guidelines on how to manage your shadow and cope much more effectively with life. Give it a read, and embrace your own inner gargoyle!

Retraining My Brain

It's been two years now since my father passed away, and though I still shudder sometimes at how difficult the many years of caregiving and witnessing my parents' suffering were, I remind myself that there is peace now, for me and for them. I'm finally focusing on the positive and moving forward.

After many years of being in that space where the proverbial shoe could drop at any time—and it did, over and over—I spent months after my father passed living in the shadow of that shoe. One day, I took the shoe down in my mind, and threw it away. Sometimes it takes a concerted conscious effort to move out from under a dark cloud that's been over your head for a long time, even if the situation no longer exists.

I often read that what you focus on expands, and it has taken conscious effort over the last two years for me to turn my focus from those difficult times to what's good and what's possible now in my life. Being stuck in a difficult and overwhelming situation for so long made my brain develop the habit of focusing on the next problem, the emotional pain that came frequently and deeply, the inevitable suffering of people who were essentially being kept alive by medication. I had to expend some effort to change that habit to focusing on peace.

And I've had to remind myself to focus on the positive. Over the last year, as I've worked on developing this new habit, I've noticed a profound change. The past is fading into a shadow of what it was, which is as it should be. And my enthusiasm and happiness is growing as I pursue some of the things I've chosen to have at the forefront in the next phase of my life.

What you focus on expands. What you think about is what you get. There's a time for letting go of the old and beginning to spend your energy and focus on what's next. For some people, that happens naturally, but having grown up in a dysfunctional family where we always focused on the negative, I had to retrain my brain in order to consciously create that process for myself.

Being There for Yourself

Growing up in a dysfunctional family, I learned that I had to be there at any time for whoever needed me, but that I could never expect anyone to be there for me. For much of my adult life, I didn't expect others, or the Universe, to support me, because I didn't know it was an option. My life's work seemed to be taking care of others.

Because of my history, most of the people I connected with wanted my attention without giving anything back. I was a dedicated codependent, and I attracted needy people.

Many self-help books and lots of self-examination later, I realized that since I'd grown up in a family where everyone expected support and encouragement to come from outside themselves, I'd never learned how to support and encourage myself from within.

So I embarked on a journey of learning how to be there for myself. Instead of pushing myself to do more and more and more, even when I was tired, I allowed myself to rest, and told myself I'd done enough. Instead of jumping down my own throat and blaming myself when things didn't work out the way I wanted, I began accepting that sometimes life throws us a curve ball, and we grow by figuring out how to deal with difficult situations. I even gave myself mental gold stars when I finished complicated projects or moved forward in a positive direction. Over time, encouraging myself made a difference, and now I know I can be there for me, no matter what.

Oddly enough, once I started encouraging myself, I found that other people began encouraging me, too. I have a great friend now who's even better at encouraging me than I am! And as I've started feeling more supported, I'm more willing to offer my gifts and talents to the world, which means I'm getting even better at everything I do, and receiving even more encouragement. It's a win-win situation.

Even small steps, like saying "That's the way," as we would to a child, can build up over time to create more confidence and self-esteem. Letting go of blaming ourselves, and discovering our competence, also makes it easier to drop the codependent habit, because then we don't feel like we have to make others happy or meet all of their expectations in order to be liked and respected.

You can learn to be there for yourself, even if no one has ever been there for you. Give yourself as much encouragement as you can, and take care of your body when it lets you know it needs attention.

You're the only person you can truly count on to be with you for the rest of your life.

Finding My Own Rhythm

When I was small, my mother was always moving: cooking, cleaning, talking, asking questions, wanting agreement, making suggestions, demanding attention, going here, going there. And when I was an adult, she was always controlling the conversation: making statements, changing the subject, asking questions, changing the subject, directing the conversation this way and that, changing the subject, until I couldn't think. She smoked and drank a lot of coffee, and the tempo at which she lived her life was too fast for me. I've recently figured out that my own best rhythm of living life is quite a bit slower.

When I was small, and moving at a pace that was too fast for me, I didn't really have time to process everything that went on. I never learned how to develop my own rhythm. I still tend to get caught up in everything there is to do, in all the learned lists of how things are supposed to be and the demands and shoulds that I grew up with, and often I try to do it all according to the rhythm I learned, instead of my own innate rhythm. Sometimes, I manage to slow down and find some peace, and that's when I realize that most of the time, I've still been living life in my mother's rhythm, even though she passed away several years ago.

It's taken quite a bit of conscious effort to break the old habitual rhythm and find my own. I have to really pay attention to what's going on when I feel overwhelmed, and stop and ask myself what I need in order to get back into my own rhythm. Usually, all I need to do is sit down for a few minutes and do nothing, and that gets my body-mind-spirit reconnected. Then I can get back to whatever I was doing, in a much more comfortable way.

The world goes so fast now, it's more important than ever to find our own rhythms so we don't get lost in the chaos of too-much-too-fast. Getting lost in the chaos and going too fast often results in getting close to the end of life and then finding ourselves wondering whether we truly lived.

What's Under the Anger Pile

A few days ago, I woke up angry. It happens sometimes. As I process some of the old memories from my dysfunctional childhood, my psyche lets some of the feelings attached to those memories bubble up into my conscious mind. If I let my body express them by stomping my feet or jumping around or punching the couch pillows (I dust them off and plump them up afterwards so nobody knows), the anger fades, and I get a little bit more clarity about where I want my life to be. The old stuff doesn't get in my way so much anymore.

I've been doing this work for a lot of years, and working on my own to sort through all of the emotions I never got to express as a child. My mother was the only one in our family who could have feelings. No one else was allowed, and so an awful lot of stuff got stuffed inside, and once it started coming out, I couldn't stop it.

Nor did I want to. The stuff I repressed got in the way of relationships, work, earning money, and feeling good about myself. It wouldn't let me succeed, it wouldn't let me be happy, it wouldn't let me be me. So I did the work of uncovering all the old stuff, and I found out what's under the anger pile.

What's under it is me. The real me that never got a chance to grow, to explore, to love, to be free. Under all of the anger and sadness and pain attached to the past, there's a happy, healthy person beginning to emerge.

The work of overcoming a dysfunctional childhood is so very hard. But it is so very worth it in the end.

Living Someone Else's Deprivation

Every now and then, I come across a belief-and-behavior pattern I inherited from my parents that is so huge and has such far-reaching consequences throughout my life history that I'm amazed once again at the power of the psyche to hide ourselves from ourselves, and the power it has to create our reality in spite of our best efforts to fashion life the way we want it.

I've written before about the situation that psychologists call "projection," where one person takes on a behavior or pattern that another denies. A prime example is a parent calling a child stupid because the parent feels vulnerable in the face of problems: the child may carry the projection of "being stupid" throughout life, regardless of his level of intelligence, and consequently never reach for anything higher than he was taught he could achieve. By projecting his or her vulnerability on the child, the parent gets to feel powerful and in control. But it can destroy the child's potential for a fulfilling and productive life.

In the psychological work that I've done, I've uncovered many facets of myself that are not part of who I really am—these are "projections," or parts of my parents' selves that they wanted to deny, and consequently "trained" me to incorporate into my life.

My parents both grew up in very poor households, but my father found a way to go to college, and he became an engineer—a white-collar worker who earned an excellent living. But he and my mother never faced their feelings of deprivation from childhood, so they projected their fears of deprivation onto me. They let me know through their words and unspoken behaviors that because I was the youngest, I was the poor one.

My mother used to give me her spare change in a Blessing Box, which is a small box that churches use to collect money for the poor. When I was older, she gave me her castoff clothing, which was occasionally torn or stained. My father used to offer me small amounts of money, then take weeks to follow through, or never send it. Through the power of these unspoken messages, I was designated "the poor one" in my family.

Over the years, I've worked to bring these old beliefs into my consciousness and let go of them, as I wrote about in my memoir, *The Box of Daughter*. By paying attention to the contrast between who I was taught I should be and who I feel I am deep inside, I've thrown off the old projections that I'm supposed to be poor, unlovable, incompetent, and deprived. My self-esteem and confidence has grown, and my life has improved immensely.

All it takes is asking yourself the question: "Is this really me? Is it really a part of who I am?" and listening for an answer that feels true. With a little time and attention, you can let go of the negative beliefs and behaviors that you learned early on, and rediscover your authentic self.

Inferior? Who, Me?

As the child of emotionally abusive parents, I have felt inferior to 99% of the population for most of my life.

The spoken and unspoken messages from my parents sat right in the middle of my psyche, taunting me every time I tried to better myself or my life: "You're not good enough!" "Who do you think you are?" "You can't do that!" "You're not worth anything!"

Even after years of therapy, those little gremlins pop up every now and then, usually when I'm about to make a big leap forward in my life. But recently, I discovered that those messages aren't part of who I am at all.

My parents were masters at projection and bullying— putting me down and shaming me so that they felt better, bigger, more powerful. They were good people, and in public, they were absolutely polite and helpful to everyone, but they dumped a lot of their inferior feelings on me because they wanted to see themselves as "perfect" people.

I know in my deepest self that they never saw me for who I really am, and that all of the put-downs were intended to make them feel better. Those messages do not define who I am. They're simply a costume my parents gave me to wear so they didn't have to face their own shame, their own feelings of weakness and vulnerability.

People who need to be perfect often feel very inferior inside—and when they're abusive and put their children down, they are transferring their own sense of inferiority onto their children. It doesn't mean in any way, shape, or form that their children are inferior.

So if your parents put you down and belittled you, the inferiority or unworthiness you probably feel does not belong to you. It belongs to them. Maybe it's time you gave it back, and started living your life from the depths of who you really are.

Letting Go of the Victim Mentality

A few days ago, a friend of mine put me down.

"That's an old idea," she said blithely. "Nobody's interested in that anymore."

For some people, a little put-down wouldn't be a big deal. But after living with constant criticism from my parents for almost five decades, the comment triggered old emotions and threw me into a tailspin.

For the rest of the afternoon, I felt as small as an ant.

Even though my parents have passed away, leftovers from dysfunctional family life still occasionally stop me in my tracks. A certain tone of voice, a particular situation, even a physical gesture that reminds me of one of my parents can trigger an old issue, throwing me back into that helpless, hopeless state I popped in and out of for almost fifty years.

Therapy has helped me distinguish between the perceptions I adopted from my parents and what is real in my world as an adult. Days, months, years of further work on my own has helped me learn how to reclaim myself after a triggering event occurs. But still, all of my nerves seem to hang out on the surface of my skin, waiting to be plucked. And my amygdala, the primitive part of the brain, often reacts before I can even think clearly about a situation.

I am what Michael Jawer and Marc Micozzi call a "thin-boundary person" in their groundbreaking book, *The Spiritual Anatomy of Emotion.* The experience of emotional abuse is part of what has made me who I am.

But therein lies the rub. For as long as I identified myself as a victim of abuse, that label was the primary ground of my being. With that identity foremost in my mind, I couldn't live authentically; I couldn't take the reins of my life and move forward into my potential. Every time I tried to do something new, I fell back into the old mantra, "I'll never get anywhere." Allowing my identity as an abused person to fade into the background has made room for profound change in my life.

For years, I coddled my pain, living in the shadow of my history. The pain was familiar; the sense of identity fostered by the false self filled the void that was created by the lack of mirroring I experienced in childhood.

One day, I woke up and decided that I didn't want to identify myself based on my wounds any longer. Realizing that my "victim identity" was stuck to me like superglue, and that I used it as an excuse for not moving forward in my life, I began to ask myself, "Beyond my experience of abuse and the difficulties it's caused in my life, who am I? And who can I become if I no longer identify myself primarily in that way?"

As I unraveled the tapestry of negative childhood messages and examined them one by one, I began to perceive myself differently. I was able to name the old messages as projections from my parents—the weaknesses, faults, and characteristics that they didn't want to recognize in themselves.

I saw that my "victim identity" was largely constructed from the fears and insecurities my parents had projected onto me, rather than being a genuine part of who I am. This insight encouraged me to dig more deeply inside to unearth more of my authentic self.

My parents were perfectionists. My childhood was filled with rules, and I was compelled to shape myself into the role of the Good Little Girl, to live in a box labeled "daughter," in order to be safe. Deep within me lies the energy of an independent spirit, a leader, an entrepreneur; but for most of my life, I was a follower out of necessity, strictly adhering to the rules laid out for me by my parents so that I could feel safe.

After my parents died, and I began to experience more freedom, I discovered that in order to be myself and create a life that works for me, I would have to consciously and determinedly disobey practically every message my parents gave me. Because I witnessed family violence in childhood, the idea of disobeying my parents is particularly challenging for me.

Whereas most people learn in adolescence that they can disobey without being violently hurt, it took me 30 years of adult living before I could allow myself to disobey the unspoken messages that I was supposed to be helpless, weak, and incapable, unsuccessful, unhappy, and poor. It took a conscious act of will to make the choice that I could disobey, and then give myself permission to be capable, happy, and successful.

In spite of practicing affirmations for many years, I couldn't move forward and create the life I wanted until I mustered the courage to disobey my parents' messages. After all, when an affirmation such as, "I am strong and confident," knocks up against an unspoken childhood message of "You're supposed to be weak and uncertain," it can't gain any power. But if a person can unravel parental messages and find the courage to consciously disobey them, the affirmation finds space in the psyche to grow.

What's tough about making the decision to disobey and move forward is the psyche's emotional reaction to choosing a different path. Throughout my journey of healing, the primary thrust of my work has been a willingness to explore any emotions that arise, to act as a witness for myself as I express them, and find a physical outlet for them. Sometimes people are unwilling to take on this kind of work, but I believe it's essential if we want to heal our pain.

Every time I made a choice to disobey an old decree, I faced old feelings bubbling up from my unconscious, seeking acknowledgment and release. Though grieving has been a primary emotion in my healing, my expression of rage has turned out to be even more important.

When I was home alone and the rage billowed up from inside, I tore up newspapers, I punched sofa pillows, I whacked my bed with an inflatable red bat, which, sadly, developed a leak pretty quickly and deflated. Over time, I was amazed at how much rage I had held inside, but I realized that after fifty years of pushing it down and hoping it would go away, I had stored quite a lot of it.

I know I will always bump up against old issues, that my bodymind's experience of the past will never completely go away. The two excellent therapists I worked with over the years, who helped me unravel the dysfunction in my family and unearth the essence of who I am, offered essential support without which I would not have made much progress.

But without my commitment to working on my own outside of therapy—through my willingness to feel and think for myself, and endeavoring to believe and behave in different ways—I doubt that I would have come so far in my journey. And through working on my own, my healing has become an integral part of who I am today—and who I am becoming—not just an hour-long event that happens once a week in a therapist's office.

Joan Didion wrote in *Slouching Towards Bethlehem*, "The willingness to accept responsibility for one's own life is the source from which self-respect springs." When you begin to let go of the victim mentality, you take the first step into responsibility for your journey of healing, the first step on the road to a more authentic life.

Getting to the Heart of the Anger

The anger in our culture spills over into every aspect of our lives: road rage, bullying, domestic violence, warfare, corporate competition. We're not supposed to notice, let alone express, our anger. But when it hides under the surface, it distorts and deforms our relationships, our careers, and our sense of who we are. It holds us back from getting what we want out of life.

For many years, I carried a huge burden of anger related to my childhood. I spent years sorting through the negative messages I'd received, and unearthing the foundation of my authentic self.

As I focused on the process of releasing my anger, I eventually learned that anger is simply "thwarted intention": when a child wants love, or needs to self-express, to have those intentions frequently blocked—even by well-meaning parents—creates a pile of frustration and anger in the bodymind which grows ever larger over time if it's not expressed.

Children who are repeatedly thwarted in their attempts to self-express often end up with depleted self-esteem, minimal motivation, and feelings of helplessness and hopelessness. In short, they grow up not knowing how to apply themselves with intention to create what they want in life. I sure know how that feels, and I imagine a lot of other people do, too.

When we permit ourselves to acknowledge and express our anger, the "pile-up" of negative feelings about self and the world starts to diminish, allowing new perspectives and possibilities which can generate positive changes in behavior. This is the way out of helplessness and hopelessness. By following the thread of the anger back to its original source, and allowing the anger to express freely in a healthy manner, a seeker begins to understand why life appears to be the way it is (hint: we learn our worldview by mimicking someone else's, or we believe what they taught us about ourselves and the world without investigating for ourselves whether it's true or not).

When the source of the anger is understood and enough of the old feelings are released, the natural force behind the anger can be transmuted into intention. When the anger is fully expressed over time, the powerful energy that was used first to deny that it existed, then to facilitate its expression, still remains. This energy can be transformed into strength of purpose, power of intention to shape life the way we want it to be.

So, get angry! Punch that punching bag! Pound an old pillow! Find a healthy way to release your anger, and allow its energy to transform into intention, passion for what you believe in, enthusiasm for the adventure of seeking what you want. If you trust your body to release the stored-up energy in a natural way, then you can use it for a natural purpose—creating a life that you love.

Expect the Best

Growing up in a very dysfunctional family, I learned early in my life not to have high expectations.

As a consequence, my ideas didn't often pan out. I guess I figured that if I didn't expect much, I wouldn't be disappointed. But instead, I ended up being disappointed most of the time.

As a child, I watched my mother begin each new project with eagerness and enthusiasm, hoping for success. But her expectations for a positive outcome diminished over time until she ended up believing that no good would come from her efforts, and so it usually didn't. Somewhere along the way, I learned to mimic her low-expectation behavior, as I imagine she had learned to mimic her own mother's point of view.

But I've recently discovered that a little enthusiasm can carry a plan or project to even greater heights than expected.

Many women (and quite a few men who grew up in dysfunctional families) were taught in childhood not to expect very much—especially in our careers and life work. When I grew up in the 1950s and '60s, many women were still being programmed to support men in achieving their goals, rather than to anticipate fulfillment of their own professional dreams.

Some of us were set up to see ourselves as second best, to have low expectations regarding position, salary, and peer respect, to disparage ourselves and our efforts rather than valuing what we do and expecting others to value it as well. A certain percentage of women have overcome the old negative messages, achieving a high position in their chosen field. I applaud their chutzpah!

But some of us have an ideal of perfection that keeps us striving to overcome our unconscious feelings of being second best, even to the detriment of our mental and physical health. And the pursuit of perfection itself can be a result of low expectations: when we don't expect much return for what we do, we're driven to try harder, do more, try anything to make it happen.

How different would our lives be if we expected to achieve our goals easily, instead of picturing our dreams at the far end of a long road of struggle? And I wonder: is there a connection between high expectations and confidence, between low expectations and low self-esteem?

Maureen Dowd said, "The minute you settle for less than you deserve, you get even less than you settled for." I resolve to raise my expectations so that they're in line with my dreams. I encourage you to do the same. By expecting the best, you immediately create the possibility that it will happen.

Clearing the Old Clutter

I've been fighting that old demon, clutter.

Somehow, the mail has piled up until it's grown to the size of a small mountain. My pile of paperwork-to-do is demanding that I pay attention to it. The echoes of their insistence follow me everywhere. I feel completely overwhelmed by my clutter.

And then it hits me: that's exactly the feeling I had when I was growing up! My family of origin was defined by a very chaotic energy, and every time I felt like I had finally figured things out, everything changed, and whatever I had organized in my head got blown away.

I always thought life was supposed to be clear and organized, planned and ordered. But it doesn't always happen that way, especially for those of us who grew up in dysfunctional families.

Where I got lost in my current struggle with clutter was in being reminded of the chaos in childhood, when I was helpless to do anything about it. Nothing I did as a child made any difference. I tried for years to make sense of it, and finally I gave up. And I carried that old belief into adulthood.

But as an adult, I do have the power to make changes in my life, to clear the old clutter. Once I realized that I was responding to the piles and their demanding voices the same way I responded to my mother when things got chaotic so many years ago, I could remind myself that now is now—it is not then—and now I have the power to clear the clutter.

Once I let go of the old way of being, I felt a burst of energy, and dug into the piles. Though it's taken a few hours, spread over the course of several days, I've reduced the pile to a very manageable size. It feels good to overcome the chaos. It feels even better to know that the problem was caused by my responding to my current situation in an old way.

Sometimes it helps to look backward to see whether something from the past is clouding your vision in the present. I don't even hear my piles now, and the silence is blessed.

Whose Worldview Have You Got?

Is the way you see the world the way it really is?

As we grow up, we buy into the collective reality because we don't know that things can be any other way. We base our view of the world on what our parents and others around us teach us to believe. But that view can only control our reality until we work on changing our perspective.

Imagine how two people with different worldviews would experience an unexpected gift coming into their lives. If one of them is used to unexpected gifts being wonderful things, that person will take it in stride, and enjoy and appreciate it. But perhaps the other person grew up with a worldview where gifts only come with strings attached or some kind of "payment" later on. For that person, the gift will create anxiety and the fear of being subject to another's agenda or of being expected to repay the gift somehow, even if that's not the giver's intention.

The reason most of us have difficulty manifesting the reality we choose is not that we're not good at it. The problem is that we haven't cleared away the old beliefs we were taught. We operate under our parents' worldview as adults, constantly recreating the old reality on a subconscious level, even if we don't like it. And if we grew up in a dysfunctional family, our views of reality can be really skewed.

Until we consciously change our perspective by digging into the beliefs that we were taught and discarding those that don't align with our current value system, life won't change much. We may work and work in an attempt to create a different reality, but we can't create something new when all the old roadblocks are still standing in the way.

If you're not happy with your life, and want to work on changing your perspective, Alice Miller's book *For Your Own Good*, is a good place to start.

The Blender Effect

This week, I feel like I'm living in a blender. Everything is whirling and twirling in a messy goo of missed appointments, half-baked emotions, unexpressed desires, and fretful annoyances. I bend uneasily under the heavy weight of my calendar, stumbling only half-effectively from one task to the next, while the clock continues tsk-ing out its count of the seconds I no longer have available to get too many things done.

The creatures on my to-do list are whining with dismay at having been left alone too long, each one moaning louder in my mind when I attend to another, in the hopes that it will become the next accomplishment.

And the accomplishments slide under my feet like a muddy, uneven treadmill, sometimes so fast that I don't even notice; and while the accomplishment treadmill chugs tiredly onward beneath my feet, the guilt-for-not-getting-enough-done movie plays over and over in my head, following the endless dog-eared loop that circles around the head of nearly every average American citizen.

The world is tilting, and I feel as if everything is about to slide off—all that I think I know about myself and life is sliding sideways into a huge confusing jumble of mistakes and missteps and misunderstandings, pushed over the edge by the scorekeeping judge of my general ability to cope with life—the critic who lives in my head and always knows where my most tender vulnerabilities lie. I look at the smoldering, sodden heap of what I thought I knew, and the sigh that starts in my brain glides slowly and steadily all the way down to my toes.

Perhaps spirituality is not always about reaching for the clouds or finding inner peace. Sometimes it's about scrabbling down into the dark earth of life, coping with the Blender Effect without resistance, and knowing that everything will still turn out okay in the end.

The End of Struggle

I've found a way to make life easier.

I've written before on the drama addiction—the fact that because I grew up in a dysfunctional family where there was a lot of tension and conflict, I have a tendency to fall into feeling like there's conflict all around me even when there isn't. Because struggle was a part of my life from day one, sometimes I unthinkingly create drama in my mind because it feels like "home." I forget that things can be easy, that life can go smoothly, and that I can get what I want.

I've recently discovered one of the ways I keep the drama addiction alive in my life. There's a part of me that resists everyday tasks, things that we need to do to keep life going—washing dishes, cleaning, keeping things in order—because I would rather be expressing my creative energy and having fun.

I call that part of me the "I don't want to" aspect of my personality. And that's the part of me that creates struggle. "I don't want to" loomed large in my childhood, as my parents tugged on each other, and on me, to get what they wanted. My parents certainly role-modeled an "I don't want to" quality when it came to meeting my needs.

The way around "I don't want to" can be summed up in one word: willingness. My practice of late is to be willing to give myself completely to everything I do, and suddenly, the struggle is gone. Things move forward smoothly and easily, I find more joy in what I do, and not surprisingly, I have more energy to nourish that part of myself that used to say, "I don't want to."

My parents were deeply committed to service in the community—their willingness manifested in their volunteering and giving to others. But at home, the "struggle against" was pervasive because they never learned in their own dysfunctional families how to nourish themselves and other family members.

Practicing an attitude of willingness allows my mind to open. Instead of being lost in thoughts of "I don't want to be doing the dishes," my mind is free to spin pictures of what I want to create in my life, to reflect on some of the issues in my life and how I might rise above them, and even to anticipate the joy of discovering new ways to have fun and take care of myself.

When "I don't want to" shows up, it reminds me that I need to nourish myself—that I need to open myself to the good things in life, to have fun and express my creative spirit. It's a clue to what I'm missing, and when I let go of the struggle, I can allow myself the freedom to enjoy.

Willingness is not easy, but it's a spiritual practice that has put me much more deeply in touch with myself and with the workings of the Universe. And my life has not only gotten easier, but enlightenment flows in effortlessly. It has opened a new door into my mind, into my soul.

Not Quite Me, Not Quite You

A Rumination, originally published in *The Meandering Muse*

Do you ever wake up in the middle of the night, in your own home, and suddenly, it's not familiar? You know what it looks like—there's the bed, that's my dresser, those are the two windows that look out on the front lawn—but you don't feel like it's yours, it's somebody else's.

I used to think it meant I had fallen into some deep form of the Power of Now, as if I was so steeped in this moment of reality that all of my memories—my deepest sense of who I was and how I'd lived—had died away into an existential nothingness.

In the middle of the night sometimes, you feel your life around you.

Sometimes you're glad you're there.

Sometimes you wish for more.

Who are we really? An inimitable collection of thoughts, desires, feelings, and behaviors, arising from the clear, true impulses of the soul and oozing up through the primordial brainstem to get trapped and muddled in the miasmic web of childhood indoctrination?

My pen sears the paper as I try to scribble away the scars of my childhood.

~

When I was small, my parents criticized me endlessly:

"Get your elbows off the table!"

"Don't talk with your mouth full."

"Change your clothes. That looks trashy."

"Pull in your tummy!"

Parts of me went away when it happened, so there have always been blank spaces in who I am, even while I continued to function: to love, to eat, to work, to play. Parts of me were always somewhere else.

But lately, they've been coming back at 4 a.m.

~

What happens to those parts we leave behind? Do they swim, untethered, in the deepest layers of our cells, drifting in the sea of consciousness, bewildered molecules of who we were and who we're meant to be, waiting for their chance to come alive?

~

I am angry today. I don't know why. Nothing has happened to produce my mood.

It's one of them—the unlived selves—a fragment lost in time and space because there was no room for it to grow. It wants out; it wants to tell me what it needs and how it felt and where it wants to go. It wants to shout its fury. It wants to live, to move my limbs and make my choices, to be a part of who I am becoming.

~

It wants me; it wants to *be* me. Like my mother did.

~

What happened to the infant me, that pure, sweet breath of bright new life who knew no pain, who lay there crying, lonely, while Mommy cleaned the kitchen?

Is she this me who wakes at 4 a.m. and doesn't recognize my life?

~

I reach out my hand, and welcome her into my heart.

~

At school, I hid behind my glasses, pretending I knew what the world was all about. The memories of fists and belts hid deep inside where I hoped no one could see them. And then one day, I put the memories so far away I didn't see them anymore myself.

~

So many parts of me got left behind. But they're still living somewhere deep inside, waiting for their turns.

~

Someday, if I wake up in the middle of the night often enough, all of me will be here.

Living in Layers

This morning, I woke early at the insistence of my cat, and lay in bed listening to the pulse of the rain coming lighter, then heavier, as the birds who were waking with the sun provided a background of sweet harmony.

I was struck by the fact that as a child I learned to focus on the world in a very linear fashion: looking at and thinking about one thing at a time, going in a single direction, accomplishing one task before I started another. This early morning experience was quite different. I was experiencing layers of life rather than a single line of it—the rain and the birds and the breeze coming in the window and the experience of my skin against the soft sheets were all interwoven with the environment I live in, my thoughts and hopes and dreams and sensations of possibility, all shifting and moving and weaving in a tremendous expression of life force energy.

The trees were moving outside the window, the flowers in the garden reaching for the light and soaking in the water to nourish themselves, the breeze taking branches in one direction, then another, while somewhere in the community other people were waking up or walking dogs, and other places across the country the skies were clear. And the experience of who I am and who I have been and who I hope to be threads through it all...

Life is such a different experience when we open up to the layers of what's happening around us. I think this must be how animals experience life—the smells intermingled with what they sense all around them in every direction, with a constant check of wind and weather and possible predators or prey.

The bonus for living in layers is that it leaves much less room for what Buddhists call "monkey mind," less room for our focus to get caught on a single thought that batters us about the laundry list of things yet to be done. Living in layers allows a more organic experience of body-mind-spirit without the domination of the mind pushing us to go in particular directions. It's a nice rest for the soul.

Universe on the Wall

One of my favorite things to do when I need to relax and connect with All That Is is watching the patterns that the sun shining through leaves makes on the wall. The branches outside the window dance if there's a slight breeze, and on the wall, the leaves turn into a three-dimensional kaleidoscope of fluttering shadows, prompting a feeling of endless time and space, infinity right there on the wall.

Some of the branches are still, and some are wafting in the breeze; some are clearly outlined, and some are fuzzy, depending on their placement; and all of them together create a flowing painting full of the wonder of nature's design. It's like watching a fire in a fireplace. If I focus on the show for awhile, I begin to feel as if I'm right there with Cosmic Intelligence, as if it's showing me its inner workings as it grows the trees and feeds the leaves, moving and shifting and changing and recreating the world around its center.

After years of watching this natural display, it only takes a few minutes now for me to shift into a very meditative state. My body knows that it's time to slow down and unite with the very fabric of life, and my mind quickly empties of daily concerns and worries. I often use this time to work on manifesting what I want in my life.

It's as if by spiraling into the shadows, witnessing the energy behind the energy that creates the Universe, I can more easily send my own energy into fulfilling my desires, whether for myself or for the good of all. The Universe on the Wall always puts me into a good space, and the rest of the day goes well.

Finding your own way to connect with Source is an important part of living a comfortable and peaceful life. You might want to check out the Universe on the Wall when you get a chance.

Giving and Receiving

I grew up with parents who were very emotionally needy. I imagine that they didn't get much love when they were small, and when they had kids, for whatever reason, they looked to us for their comfort and love and attention, rather than seeking it from each other.

As a result, I didn't get much emotional nourishment myself. I grew up being a "giver," but never learning much about how to receive. I truly believe in giving, but if we don't know how to let ourselves be nourished, we can quickly become very burned out.

In my ongoing work to let go of the past and move forward in my life, I recently discovered that my energy is still flowing "outward" almost continuously: flowing out into working, sustaining my relationships, and creating a fulfilling life for myself. Even when I stop to relax (which isn't as often as it should be), I'm thinking about the next wave of giving outward, instead of taking in nourishing energy. I get tired and cranky before I know it, and usually wait until I'm exhausted before I rest.

I thought back into my past. What caused this habit to develop? I remembered that when things got rough in my family, I shut myself off from everything that was happening—and now I realize how much of life I'm still shutting out. There is so much beauty and bounty in the world, if we only stop to take it in! At this point, I'm starting to "retrain" myself to let it in, to allow it to nourish me.

So if you've always been a "giver," take some time for yourself in your life—to stop, be still, to allow the Universe to nourish you. We all deserve nourishment, even if we were taught those many years ago that we didn't. And if you give it permission, the Universe is happy to provide.

How to Get More of What You Want

Doesn't it feel good when you get what you want? Want to know how to get more of that feeling?

A slight diversion into the realm of dysfunctional family patterns is necessary in order to weed out the roots of what holds us back from getting what we want. When we're children, we're growing our brains and personalities, and we want everything we can get our hands on. "Mine!" we say. "Mine!" That's normal—it's part of how we learn about the world around us.

What happens when the adults who are in charge begin to teach us that we can't have everything we want (also a normal part of the growing-up process) is that our partially developed brains can eventually register this information as "I hardly ever get anything I want." Carrying this belief system into adulthood is a major obstacle to creating a life that we enjoy, and to getting what we want.

What we need to do in order to get more of what we want is to re-train our brains. This is why affirmations often only work to a certain degree: with affirmations, we attempt to reprogram our brains with words and concepts, whereas the original imprinted information was also related to actions and behavior.

Bodies remember even more than minds do. And in fact, most children understand actions and behavior more than they understand words and concepts, because we spend the first year or two of our lives in nonverbal, language-less awareness. So we need to incorporate actions and behavior into the work of reprogramming the brain.

One way to do this is to make a practice of telling yourself "I can get what I want" before you do something that you know you're going to get. If you're going out to dinner, tell yourself, "I want to go out to dinner" before you go. Then remind yourself afterwards, "I got what I wanted. Therefore, I can get what I want." It sounds silly, but in essence, you're reprogramming your brain—when you repeat this experience over and over—by creating an affirmation that is true for you in the moment, one that you can feel and experience on every level of your being (physical, emotional, spiritual, mental).

Sometimes affirmations can make what you're trying to manifest seem far off in the future, like "I am now wealthy, healthy, and happy." The trick to reprogramming your brain is to affirm something *when it happens in the moment*, and then decide that it can continue, and expand it into your future.

When you receive money for something, affirm right then and there, "It is easy for me to receive money," or whatever phrase works for you. When you receive love or admiration or a compliment from someone, affirm to yourself, "I am lovable and worthy," and let your imagination carry that feeling into the future.

If it helps, you can say, "In this moment, I am lovable and worthy." Just make sure you expand that feeling, and send thoughts of receiving it again (or receiving even more) into the next week, month, or year.

Mostly, this practice just requires paying attention in the moment when you receive something you want.

When you wake up feeling down or tired, no matter how many affirmations you say, you are sending your manifestation the energy of "down" or "tired." The time to affirm is when you're feeling great and already getting at least a bit of what you want—at that moment, it's very easy to believe you can manifest what you desire.

This runs a little contrary to the way we think affirmations should work, because when we're in a great mood, or getting what we want, we don't think about creating more of it. But this is exactly the time to create more of it—to expand that good feeling, to extend those good thoughts, to send that energy out into the Universe to create more of what you want.

Nourish Your Divinity

In dysfunctional families, we often learn the codependent pattern of "taking care of others." The implication is that if we take care of others, others will take care of us. But what often ends up happening is that nobody feels fulfilled, and the cycle of trying to take care of others goes round and round until we want to fall down with exhaustion. At least I always did.

The reason that taking care of others doesn't work is that no one knows what another person needs to feel nourished (unless they can tell us clearly and directly, and in dysfunctional families, they usually don't). We end up guessing: "Oh, I think this would help." "It seems to me that he needs that." But we can't guess what would truly nourish another person. He or she may not even know themselves.

The other side of the codependent coin is not being able to nourish ourselves. We're so busy trying to meet the unknown needs of others, we don't have time or focus or energy left for ourselves. We may not even be aware of our needs.

This is a dysfunctional pattern, born of misunderstanding and misinterpretation. We can't know what others truly need, but with a little investigation, we can find out what nourishes us, and place our focus there. Then we become a role model for others—when we see someone nourishing themselves, we tend to allow more space in our lives to do that for ourselves.

However, there are times in dysfunctional relationships when others don't want you to nourish yourself. Watching you take care of yourself makes them more uncomfortable with their own needs. In that case, you'll have a little push/pull, a little conflict, as they try to drag you back into taking care of them, hauling you back into the throes of Spider Love.

Don't fall for it. Go ahead and nourish yourself.

I know, I know, it makes you feel guilty. Me, too. But you are part of the Divine Consciousness, the totality of the Universe—God, or Buddha, or Higher Power—whatever you choose to call it. If you are not nourished, it's nearly impossible to do your real work in the world, to serve the purpose for which your soul came here to Earth. So when you nourish yourself, you are nourishing the energy of the Universe. You're nourishing the Divine within yourself.

Who wouldn't want to nourish God? That's what you're doing when you take care of yourself. When you begin to nourish your soul—your Divine spirit—you set foot on the path you were meant to take in this lifetime, and your purpose will reveal itself over time. When you're just "taking care of others," your purpose languishes, and the potential you have to bring the Divine creative power forth in your life to make the world a better place remains hidden.

Trust yourself. You are the only person who knows what nourishes you. Happy creating! And may the Force be with you.

Invite Yourself In

I was raised by Depression-era parents who were thrifty to a fault, the precursor generation to "Reduce, Reuse, Recycle." My father's father was a minister, and my father learned the art of self-deprivation at an early age.

As a child, I identified deeply with the Poor Little Match Girl, and decades later, I'm still trying to throw off the belief that life is supposed to be about deprivation, so I can move into a little more abundance, feel a little safer as I shuffle toward retirement.

Though my father was a white-collar worker and we always had enough, when I was small, the focus was on doing without, making do with less, and stashing every penny away in a savings account—all of which are good values, but my early training left me with the feeling that there is never enough of anything in my life.

I've read *The Secret*, books on prosperity thinking and overcoming underearning; I've even made good money in some periods of my life. But still, the feeling has persisted that there's not enough and there never will be. In the deep recesses of my mind hides the fear I've pushed away over and over, tried to tread into dust, and worked to dismantle: that one day, I will end up with nothing.

I once read that the way to move beyond the "bag lady" fear is to decide what you would need to have in your basket: a blanket, a library card, a change of clothes.... It made me feel a little more prepared, but no less fearful.

Recently I happened upon the Poor Little Match Girl again online—and suddenly a little voice (my inner child, I suppose) piped up, "Nobody ever invited us into abundance." I had to stop for a moment. She was right. My psyche has been waiting all my life for an invitation.

So last week, I sent an invitation to myself, with an RSVP. I accepted immediately, and the change is already apparent. Sometimes you have to invite yourself, if nobody else has.

The Divine Energy of the Universe doesn't know limitation. Whatever it is that you want to have in your life, this source energy can always create more of it. So, even if something seems to be lacking, more of it can always be created. We were made to live in alignment with our desires. All it takes is letting go of the old, and allowing the possibilities to unfold.

Who Do Your Parents Think You Are?

My family was so enmeshed that I still feel like I have three heads, even though my parents have been gone for almost four years.

One of my three "heads" is the voice of my mother, who often told me I was an extreme extrovert like she was (because she wanted me to be like her). Another is the voice of my father, a quiet, solitary, logical person—who, of course, thought I was just like him. My parents were complete opposites who never learned how to make room in a relationship for differences, so they both turned to me for mirroring and support.

In between those two "heads" is my own: I'm an extremely creative person who loves solitude at times, and also loves being with people. There are many other ways in which I'm different from my parents, and every time I discover a new morsel of authentic self inside, I remind myself that it's perfectly okay to be who *I* want to be, not who my parents wanted me to be.

Most of us play "roles" in our families that don't reflect the totality of who we are. In my case, I shoved about 85% of myself into some unknown, dark place whenever I had to interact with my parents, because they didn't want me to be very much different than they were.

Because my parents grew up during the Depression, the "self" that they allowed me to be was pretty limited. Consequently, over the years I've had to spend some time rummaging around inside myself to unearth more of my authentic self. The question that has helped me most often is "Who do my parents think I am?" vs. "Who do *I* think I am?"

My parents thought I was the Good Little Girl, because that's who they wanted me to be. For decades during my adult life, I was a doormat because they had trained me to be totally responsive to other people's needs with no consideration for my own. I do enjoy giving to other people, but when it's required over a very long period of time, the joy leaves, quickly replaced by total burnout.

I've come to realize that I can have a good heart and be deeply compassionate without being a doormat. And I can give to other people, as long as I give to myself as well.

So if you're in the process of excavating your authentic self, you might ask yourself: "Who do my parents think I am?" and "Who do I think I am?"

Or, even better, "Who do I want to be?"

Disaster Relief

When the earthquakes happened in Haiti a few years ago, I started thinking about how we co-create our reality.

Well-known consciousness researcher Dean Radin uses random number generators to demonstrate that when people all over the world are focused on a single event—the opening of the Olympics, for example—the shared field represented by the random number generators becomes more coherent.

In effect, all the people watching are "hooking up" with each other and affecting reality. Radin has demonstrated this effect repeatedly, in a number of different situations, and points out that although we may not be able to influence the outcomes of events very powerfully as individuals, we may be able to achieve that influence as a group or collective.

With that in mind, picture this: Shortly after the earthquake in Haiti, thousands of people are watching TV when news of the earthquake comes through. There are a few dreadful pictures, and everyone watching thinks, "Oh, how horrible!" And it is. But the energy those thousands of people are sending is fear, darkness, anxiety—and maybe that energy creates a small earthquake aftershock.

Within an hour, another million people have seen the story on the internet, all thinking, "Oh, how horrible!" Billions of fearful thought-atoms are now being focused every minute on poor Haiti and the people who are having such a hard time. And the earth (which is a field of energy just as the random number generators are) responds to that huge influx of thought-energy: there are several more aftershocks.

By that evening, billions of people are sending frightful and anxious thought-atoms to Haiti, and the situation grows worse and worse.

How would an event like this be different if, instead of sending thoughts of fear and anxiety and pity, from the moment we heard about a disaster, we began sending prayers for peace, comfort, and healing?

It's absolutely natural to react to a major disaster with fear, sadness, and anxiety, but if we spend hours or days tuning into the news media and watching an ever-growing horror—whatever it might be—we are contributing to its growth in every moment we think about it.

Sometimes I wonder if this is why we haven't yet been able to eradicate war and sustain peace: every time there's more fighting, most of our collective minds are sending out thought-waves about fighting, instead of thought-waves about peace.

Scientists have proven that we can create our own reality, and when an earthquake or other event occurs, we are creating the situation as we focus on it. As conscious beings who desire to help others and heal our planet, it would behoove us to consciously send thoughts of peace and healing as often as we can for as long as we can when a major disaster occurs.

The side benefit is that it helps us feel more peaceful, too.

Nature's Music

I think that crickets created jazz. One night in late summer a few years ago, I was sitting on the back porch enjoying the sunset, and I started listening to the rhythm of the crickets. Two of them were talking back and forth across the street. "ZZZ zzz zzz." Pause. "zzz ZZZ zzz." Pause. "Zzz."

As I listened, I noticed that they would continue in a certain rhythm of threes or fours for awhile, but then one would skip a beat, and the other would immediately moderate his or her rhythm. Once in awhile, everything would get off track and they'd be zzz-zing at the same time, or one would shut up to let the other initiate a new rhythm. (As a musician, I notice these things).

I imagined some mild-mannered old musician down in New Orleans a hundred years ago, sitting and listening to the rhythm of the crickets, and using it as a beat for his new song. They really have a sense of rhythm! And when one drops out altogether, whether to feed or mate or just rest for awhile (or whatever else crickets do), the other keeps the beat going just in case the first wants to jam some more.

What's really amazing is when three or more of them get going at once—the options for rhythm and beat counterpoint are much more complex, and when one puts a little extra beat into the mix, the other two each come up with their own new response, and they're off on a completely different riff.

Which brings me to the subject of ears: did you know that crickets have ears on their legs? I suppose that means that their response time between hearing another cricket and making their own sound is pretty fast. And I always want to know the purpose of things. Why were crickets created? Sure, they eat bugs, but maybe their intended purpose was to create jazz so that humans could copy and build on it, and sit in lounges with a glass of wine, enjoying the gift of the crickets.

Nature is truly amazing. I hope you get a chance to listen to the cricket jazz next summer.

Recommended Reading

Finding Your Own North Star: Claiming the Life You Were Meant to Live by Martha Beck

Bradshaw on the Family by John Bradshaw

Healing the Shame that Binds You by John Bradshaw

Homecoming by John Bradshaw

Soul without Shame: A Guide to Liberating Yourself from the Judge Within by Byron Brown

Are You Really Too Sensitive? by Marcy Calhoun

Subtle Energy by William Collinge, Ph.D.

Warming the Stone Child: Abandonment and the Unmothered Child—a wonderful and supportive audio recording by Clarissa Pinkola Estés, Ph.D.

Mother Night—another great supportive audio recording by Clarissa Pinkola Estés, Ph.D. which will help you build your self-esteem no matter who you are or what you believe

Toxic Parents by Susan Forward

Creative Visualization by Shakti Gawain

Ask and It is Given by Abraham Hicks

The Dance of Anger by Harriet Goldhor Lerner

The Box of Daughter by Katherine Mayfield

Stand Your Ground: How to Cope with a Dysfunctional Family and Recover from Trauma by Katherine Mayfield

The Field by Lynne McTaggart

The Drama of the Gifted Child by Alice Miller

For Your Own Good by Alice Miller

If You Had Controlling Parents by Dan Neuharth, Ph.D.

Take Charge of Your Life: How Not to Be a Victim by Louis Proto

The Empowered Mind by Gini Graham Scott

Authentic Happiness by Martin Seligman

Learned Optimism by Martin Seligman

About the Author

A former actress who appeared Off-Broadway and on the daytime drama Guiding Light, Katherine Mayfield is the author of the award-winning memoir *The Box of Daughter*; a guide to recovery from bullying for teens and adults, called *Bullied: Why You Feel Bad Inside and What to Do About It*; a book of essays, *The Meandering Muse*; a guide to writing memoir, *What's Your Story?*; a book of poetry; and several books on recovering from dysfunctional family dynamics. She has also published two books on the acting business, *Smart Actors, Foolish Choices* and *Acting A to Z*, with Back Stage Books. She has spoken at schools, libraries, and conventions on the subjects of recovery from bullying and creating an authentic life.

Ms. Mayfield's memoir *The Box of Daughter* won the Bronze Medal in the Reader's Favorite Book Awards, an Honorable Mention in the New England Book Festival, and was nominated as a Finalist in the Maine Literary Awards. *The Box of Daughter* was inspired by the title poem in her book of poems, *The Box of Daughter and Other Poems*. She blogs on dysfunctional families on her website, www.TheBoxofDaughter.com.

Websites:
www.TheBoxofDaughter.com
www.Katherine-Mayfield.com

Social Media:
Twitter: K_Mayfield
Facebook: KatherineMayfieldauthor

CPSIA information can be obtained
at www.ICGtesting.com
Printed in the USA
LVHW010936260819
628925LV00002B/70/P